LadyBirdLand!

by Allison Strine

StoryPeople Press

ISBN-13: 9780974551630
ISBN-10: 0974551635

Copyright © 2011 by Allison Strine

This book is a work of fiction. Names, characters, places, and incidents either are products of the author's imagination or are used fictitiously. Any resemblance to actual events or locales or persons, living or dead, is entirely coincidental.

All rights reserved. No part of this book may be reproduced or transmitted in any form or by any means, electronic or mechanical, including photocopying, recording, or by any information storage and retrieval system, without permission in writing from the Publisher.

StoryPeople Press
P.O. Box 7
Decorah, IA 52101
USA
563.382.8060
563.382.0263 FAX
800.476.7178

storypeople@storypeople.com
www.storypeople.com
www.storypeoplepress.com

Library of Congress Control Number: 2010941004

First Edition: February, 2011

Introduction

When I was eight, my short-tempered father and harried mother took all five of us kids on a road trip from our rambling home in Boston to Montreal for the grand spectacle of Expo '67. I'm not sure which was the sweetest vacation highlight, because they're all so vivid, forty-odd years later. First, there was the ten carsick, seat belt-less hours in the family station wagon. As the middle child, of course I got squashed in between Brian and Bradley in the back seat, being elbowed and "noogied" all along the way. Then there was the fight between me and Jennifer over whose pillow it was. That one ended with a furious father pulling over to the side of the highway in the dead of night, only to pitch said pillow out the window with a flick of the wrist. Hopefully, the other arm was on the steering wheel. Of course, being the baby of the family, Rachel got to sit in between Mom and Dad in the coveted front seat the whole way. Jealous? Who?

Oh, wait, now I remember. Undoubtedly, the most life scarring incident, one which still makes me shiver all these years later, was when my two older brothers sat on me and farted for three hours while everyone else was canoeing. Yep, good times. That's what families are made of: farting brothers and pillow-fighting sisters.

Tortured memories like these have long festered in my soul, until I finally called upon on the healing powers of art to soothe and nurture my poor ravaged heart. And that, ladies and gentleman, is the story of where LadyBirds come from. Aren't you glad you asked?

Thanks go to my amazing husband Lloyd, without whom LadyBirds would never be possible. If not for Lloyd showing me how powerful love is, I'd still be that lost little girl (but with more gray hair). Thank you to StoryPeople Press for bringing joy and good vibes into a world that needs it. Mom, don't worry - the scars have healed and it wasn't your fault anyway! Dad, I miss you and know how very proud you would have been. Brian, Bradley, Jennifer and
Rachel - thanks for being the glue that keeps our odd little family together. Finally, my biggest mommy love to the centers of my little universe, Olivia and Ethan.

-Allison Strine

Welcome to LadyBirdLand!

by Allison Strine

My sister Rachel is the sweetest girl. She has a cooking business and she's very good to her customers. They think she's gentle and meek and a doll, but then VROOOM, VROOM!! After work she puts on motorcycle leathers and goes tooling around the countryside on her big, fat motorcycle! So there! She must be a tough chick, right?

Well, I contend that we all have depths, and many of us are sugar and spice in one aspect of our lives, and everything kick ass in another. I have a friend who is the NICEST person in car pool, and she also runs marthons. You tell me she's not kick ass!

Sugar And Spice

Not that I would ever do that. Oh, no. I'm much too fashion conscious to spend the whole day wearing a grubby art tee shirt, boobs a floppin'. But this little lady would, and it makes her very happy as you can see by the size of her heart!

Braless

She doesn't look back. Hmmm. What's it mean? Well, for starters, it tells me to keep my eye on the present. Just be the best "me" that I can be TODAY. Not blaming my parents now for their past mistakes, not dwelling on the past, living in the present, and so on (ad nauseam?). This is definitely a piece of art made from my child's heart, you know?

Don't Look Back

I don't know why nobody appreciates my incredible recycling abilities. Did you not see the glint of earth-saving justice fighter in my eye? For years I was the strange lady with the big, huge LL Bean tote bags for her groceries. The one who got eye rolling, sideways leers from the baggers 'cause I was so disdainful of their stinkin' plastic.

Now that everyone's on that tote-bag kick, I've moved on to bigger and better things. Now I'm all 'bout being the best recycler in our neighborhood. We're the family with one garbage can full of trash, and two, mind you, TWO, cans full of recycle. And I'm not talking little garbage bins. We're talking full-size babies here! I'm so proud!

Or maybe, this saying is all 'bout growing up and having our best talents unnoticed. Lisa says she can do a one-handed cartwheel, but does anyone care?

Recycling

She. Must. Create. I never even knew that was an option, and now I can not imagine my life without a little me time each and every day, to make something beautiful, or not beautiful, as the case may be.

I think in this case we all are creating. Girls who love to cook, or bake, or do the house nicely, or even mix the right shoes with the right eyeshadow (something I don't do). We're all creating, right?

Must Create

Seeing life through Mom-colored glasses. To me, that means a tiny bit more worrying about things, a lot more checking to see if the kids are safe, keeping the knives up on top of the fridge, and building a tree swing in the front yard.

What about you? Do you see life through Mom-colored glasses?

Mom-Colored Glasses

I must confess that for years I didn't know what a Blackberry was. When that guy on Survivor was typing on a piece of wood, pretending it was his PDA, I still didn't quite get the excitement. So, you can email on a train. Yeah, and? I always got the cheapest cell phone available. They're all the same, right?

Until (insert schmaltzy violins here) I got my IPHONE!! OOOOH!!! SQUEAL!! DELIGHT!!! I can type! I can check email obsessively! I can find a satellite picture of my house! I can flick my finger through my calendar! Love! Squeeze!! Keep!!!

iPhone

Ooh! Ooh! Ooh! This might be my new favorite saying! I think it's all 'bout taking charge of our own moments, our lives, and making sure to find the joy whenever and wherever we can.

Here's a little example. We had all gone to get some Halloween fabric, and six-year-old Ethan wanted to get a gift card during the checkout. I always let the kids get those cards, and, in fact, Olivia had kept a collection of them for almost a year. No big deal. Anyway, we get back to the car, and Ethan is almost in tears. I asked him what was going on and he said that he had wanted to put money on the card. He must have just figured out that the cards are useless without money on them. I started to tell Ethan that it was no big deal and he should forget about it, and then I just wanted to make him happy. So I asked Lloyd to take him in the store, and they put five dollars on the card, and then when they came out Ethan gave it to me as a present. He was so happy to be able to give, and it made me change from thinking I was a crappy parent, who just gives in at the sight of tears, to thinking that maybe I helped him and me to learn a lesson about happiness!

The funny ending to the story is that I'd totally forgotten about this saying, and only found it while rummaging in the car last night. I had jotted it down on the gift card. Yay, for helping ourselves to happiness!

Helps Herself

I have always found great solace in books. My mom used to take us all to the library on Wednesdays, and we'd feed the ducks and get new books. First, it was *Harriet the Spy*. Oh my gosh, did I love that book! I read it over and over and over. I totally connected with Beverly Cleary's books too. I used to imagine I was Henry Huggins' friend. His problems were so much more fun than mine!

A zillion years later and one of my proudest parenting hoo-hahs is that both Ethan and Olivia are voracious readers. We have a picture of us walking down the street in the city of Oslo, and Ethan's reading and walking at the same time. I love that!

Book Queen

I'm struggling right now to achieve some health goals, and my healthy sister, Rachel, keeps telling me how much of a mind game the whole thing is. I know she's right, 'cause when I started in February with the right mindset, slowly but surely good things happened: weight loss, energy, feeling good, all of it. Then I tweaked my back and had to take a few weeks off from running and exercising, and now with school out and the kids home, I'm struggling to get close to the mental strength I had before.

Yesterday, I mustered up the energy for a run/walk, and realized that Rachel's right. It's ALL about the mental state. If I think I can't do it, I'm right. And without something/someone to push me, I don't know how much I could/can achieve, 'cause I would wuss out when it got uncomfortable. So I drew up this mental image with this very saying and dangled it in front of me like a carrot, and it helped me through my run. And it's gonna help me achieve my health goals!

Maybe it can help you too?

Off Her Ass

My mom and I talk on the phone each day, and nary a conversation goes by without one of us bragging on the perfection of our respective dog. She thinks Roberta is wonderful (insert eye roll here). Sure, she's sweet and all, but Roberta certainly couldn't compare to my Fern! Why, Fern follows me everywhere, worries little chew toys, and wags a lot! Sheer genius in the shape of a doggie, I say! Fern's more equal than anyone!

Equal Dog

When I was little I wanted to be Suki Bullens. She was the coolest girl in my school. Oooh, to be able to play basketball like Suki! She was such an athlete, and I even walked pigeon-toed, just so I could be like her.

Then, I wanted to be like Lauren. She was so confident. You could just tell she didn't care what anyone else thought.

All my life I wanted to be someone else, someone smarter, prettier, more athletic, funnier, more anything. Until, finally, I realized that I'd never be a good Suki, or Lauren, or anyone else. But I could be a really good Allison! So that's what I'm working on, and it's getting better and better.

Beautiful

Confession Number 462: I really have no idea what this phrase means. It's been going in and out of my head for weeks now, and I kept thinking, "Self, don't make a saying like this. It has no meaning!"

And then I'd say, "Self, this is funny, and I like it!"

And that went on for a long time, and then I gave up and turned it into a saying! I think I'm putting it in my studio. No, I KNOW I'm putting it in my studio. It might inspire me. At least it will get me thinking...

Creative Slip

Hmmmm. I wish that I could be better at this one. I want to have faith in Faith. I do love this sentiment. It seems like the right thing to do. That is, of course, after you work for your dreams, live your fabulous life, be in a creative mood, carpe the diem and live out loud. THEN I can leave the rest to God!

Or... I should leave the resting and relaxing for God to do, and do more now!!!

Rest To God

Are you doing it all? Living? Check. Loving? Definitely. Laughing? As much as humanly possible, especially at myself. Hoping? Oh, yeah, I want it ALL to work out, whatever IT is. Dreaming? Well, sometimes they're scary dreams, but sometimes they're flying dreams, and that is ALL RIGHT!

Living And Loving

Sometimes you just have to deal with life, you know? Like when there are fifteen cars in front of you at the intersection. And they're all turning left, like you are. And no one knows that you really need to get to school. That's when I sigh, hitch up my big-girl panties, and just deal with it. By the way, don't make me tell you the size of my big-girl panties. That's all I'm going to say on the subject.

Big Girl Panties

It started as an innocent little distraction, didn't it? Then the friends from high school showed up, and the people you used to work with. You missed those guys from the olden days, didn't you? And it was great to hear 'bout their lives. All those "I wonder what happened to so-and-so" questions being answered.

Then it became interesting to see what Patti Digh was having for lunch, right? It became important that the world knew when you were making coffee. Then came the applications: the Farkle, the Word Scramble, the endless trivia. It's when you come to the "wait-a-minute" stage that you know you have a problem. That's the stage where you're not available to answer a child's question because you're in the middle of taking a very important quiz.

At least that's what I've heard.

Facebook

Ooh, I do I do I DO love being a Mom! It defines a whole big chunk of me! And the perks are so great: getting to read *Go, Dog, Go!* again, having an excuse for keeping Goldfish around (geez, those things are addicting), and, of course, the warm, little bodies all around! This to remind yourself that you love being a Mom, even when your nine year-old huffs 'bout how EMBARRASSING you are... hypothetically speaking.

Being A Mom

Oh, I'm not going to tell you that in seventh grade the art teacher rapped my knuckles with a ruler for going outside the lines. Oh, no, that happened in fourth grade. Man, those teachers were tough! Now, of course, I know only the best artistes go outside the line. The further, the better!

Outside The Lines

This saying is about being okay with who we are today. Yeah, I know, there's plenty of room for self improvement, and Oprah will tell us to work harder, but I still think there's something to be said for taking a deep breath, and letting it out, and knowing that I am OK.

Good Enough

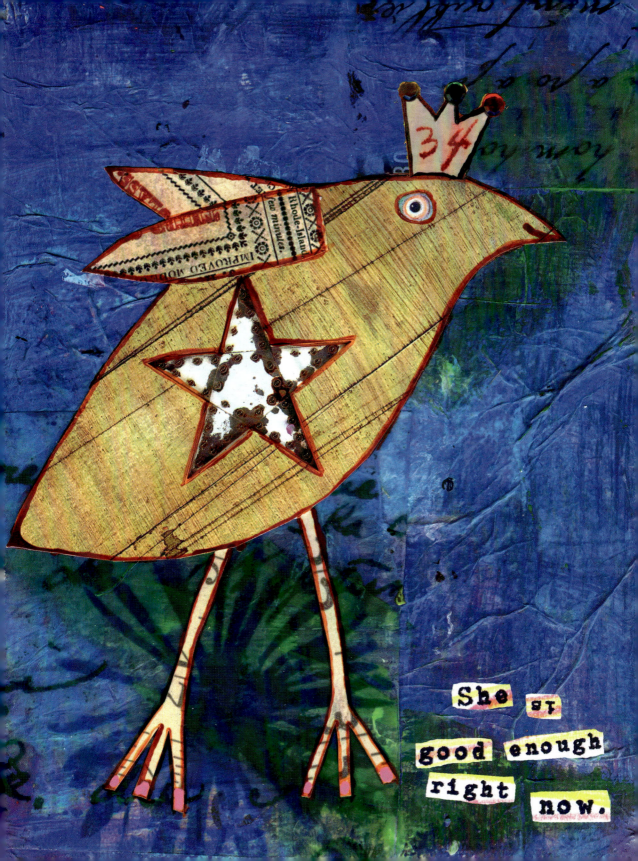

This is a bit Seuss-esque, but I am glad to be Me. Most of the Time. And I do want to believe that there's no other Me that I'd like to Be. And I want my little Olivia to feel the same way, so I have to lead by example, right?

Glad To Be She

There's a mom at my kids' school who I admire very much. She is who she is, and she knows what she knows, and she is as kind and sweet as can be, but she doesn't take anything from anyone and I love that! She has bumper stickers all over the back of her car, and one of them says something like this.

I love the saying. It's succinct, it's appropriate, and it celebrates the world of women who fit into our own darn pegs!

Fit In

Wouldn't this be the coolest thing to come true? I would dearly LOVE to be able to take a deep breath and blow all the fears and insecurities out the window. Then I'd tiptoe across the fields happy and light and freeeee! Like a tampon commercial.

But the worries and fears are part of me, and I'm thinkin' I'm kinda stuck with them. Maybe I need the magic wand to turn those insecure thoughts into dust! So this piece is to embolden and strengthen and remind me to ignore those silly scared voices!

Am I alone here?

Poof

I guess I'm feeling quite defiant today, or maybe I've been watching too much *Sex and the City*, 'cause I don't see why ANYONE has to sit around and moon over a guy, waiting for someone.

To give her hope... to carry ooonnnn.... and light up her da-ays ...and fill her nights... with sooonggg! (That was me singing. Can you tell?)

I'm giving this one to Rachel, who is wonderful enough to stand on her own two high heels, and march around with her own damn lamp! Can I get a tweet tweet?

Lights It Up

Do you imbibe? Or sip? Or guzzle? Or share with good friends? My Manischewitz history (for you gentiles, that's the wine that Jews drink at Passover) has scarred me for life so that my palate can't tell Boone's Farm from Chateau Lafitte du Pincay du Haut Rothschild Margaux Marilyn Merlot, but I do like me some cheap wine with good friends. Or is it the other way around?

Wine

Sometimes you just have to throw your hands up in the air and know that it's all going to be alright, right? That's what little Phoebe here thinks. You can't get too bogged down in the details, and the what-ifs, and the maybes... you just have to trust!

Universe

You know the Seinfeld episode where they spend the whole time trying to figure out if this gorgeous girl's breasts are real or implants? I think Jerry's dating her. And Elaine is in the sauna with the girl and she trips and stumbles right into them? And then at the very end, the proud, breast girl dumps Jerry and then smugly says, "They're real. And they're spec-tacular." And then she struts off? You know that one?

Well, we're real too, aren't we? And can't we be spec-tacular too? Why not? And can we be proud and even smug about our realness and spec-tacular-ness? We're not just about the boobies, are we girls?

Spectacular

My favorite color is every single one of them, from the darkest violets to the wildest greens to the lemony yellows! But, of course, my most favorite one of all is SPARKLE! And my favorite flavor is easy, by the way...

How 'bout you? Are you a sparkle girl too?

Sparkle

I don't know about you, but sometimes the weight of the diamonds in my tiara is just plain crushing. I have to do neck exercises just to build up the strength required to maintain my queenliness. It's a hard life, and I don't know how Elizabeth does it. Queen Liz, that is. My British compatriot.

MY life is the one that's difficult. I (emphasis on "I," if you please) am the one who scratched my impeccably-manicured fingernail opening the door of my Jag. (Really it's a Honda minivan, but I'm being British right now.) I'm too exhausted to continue. Please, excuse my rudeness. I must rest.

Tiara

I'M ALERT!!! I'M AWAKE!!! I JUST HAD MY COFFEE!!! THAT'S WHY I'M YELLING!!!!

Put the coffee cup down and step away from the keyboard.

(deep breath)

Okay, I'm fine now. I'm just feeling the jones associated with my morning java brew. Seriously, sometimes I feel like I can't create without the joe. Anyone else?

Caffeine

Last week my ten-year-old daughter Olivia's cousin came to visit from New Hampshire. Robin is almost 16, and an amazingly wonderful role model. Olivia worships Robin to the nth degree, even becoming a vegetarian just 'cause Robin's one.

Anyhoo, we took the kids to Six Flags White Water, where there are all kinds of crazy water rides. Olivia is notoriously cautious, definitely not a roller-coaster-type-of kid. Robin, on the other hand, loves that crazy adrenalin rush. You know where this story's going.

Robin talked Olivia into going down the most insanely scary, steep, one-person-drop water ride that I've ever seen. They waited in line for a really long time, and Liv didn't chicken out. She came shooting down the plunge like a petrified, green, bathing-suited streak. She was very proud of herself, and said she'd never do it again, but she did it!

See how powerful she is?

Powerful

I like big mutts and I can not lie.
You other Mothers can't deny
That when a Newfoundland-Collie-Corgi mix
Does adorable doggie tricks
You fall in love
With a small mixed breed.
He'll love you, guaranteed.

I gotta Terrier-Affenpinscher
And those brown eyes are the clincher.
I know that dog is flea full,
But that Chow Chow mix
Makes me so gleeful.

Ooh, Yorkie-Borzoi,
You wanna be my new toy?
Pug mixed wit' a Basset Hound.
I'll take you from that nasty pound.
Doggy got home.

So ladies (yeah), ladies (yeah)
Wanna pet my mutt named Sadie? (yeah)
Then grab a leash.
You're shelter bound.
Pick a lonely dog from the pound.
Doggy got home.

(With great props to Sir Mix-A-Lot for the inspiration!)

Big Mutts

What's a miracle to you? To me, some days, it seems like nothing is, and then on other days, every single thing in the world is a miracle. From my dog's expressive eyes to the fact that my car goes when I push the pedal down, miracles abound if we look for them. And I do like the little ones the best!

Miracles

I'm so confused sometimes. It's like I'm still a kid with impulses and joy and goofy grins, but then I look in the mirror, and it's like, "Damn! Where'd the old chick come from?"

Sometimes I'll act all responsible, and in charge, and know stuff, and then I'm like, "Damn! Where's the fun in that? Give me a balloon!"

Know what I mean?

Cleverly

I can't think of a better lift-yourself-up, confidence-boosting, you-go-girl saying than this one. Making the conscious decision to be worth it is tantamount to giving yourself the permission to be a confident person, to nurture and care for yourself, and best of all, to not take any shit from anyone. 'Cause, after all, you are worth it.

Worth It

About the Artist

By day, Allison is a happy artist whose irrepressible creations have been featured in fancy art magazines, and now - a book! At night she's a not-very-good cook, wife to a right-brained hunk, (or is it the left? You know, the one that's all about math and not really about art?) and the tucker-inner of two perfectly-behaved, well-groomed children. Yeah, right.

LadyBirdLand is the result of Allison's off-centered view of the world around her. Putting the "full" in full color illustration, her magically delicious collages go straight to the heart. LadyBirds have been transformed into art magnets, prints and soldered pendants for the most discerning of girls, and they can be found in glorious, gifty shops across the USA. For the internet savvy, look for LadyBirds at allisonstrine.etsy.com. Learn more about me (I mean, her) at allisonstrine.com!

About StoryPeople

StoryPeople Press is located in the heart of America (That's right... Iowa). Through its publications, StoryPeople Press strives to make the world a better place by spreading the words of laughter, imagination and inspiration. To see what other works are available, visit www.storypeoplepress.com.

StoryPeople features the the work of Brian Andreas and includes StoryPeople sculptures, colorful story prints, and books, all available in galleries and stores throughout the US, Canada and the EU (along with a few others scattered about the world), and on their web site. Please feel free to call or write for more information, or drop in on the web at www.storypeople.com

StoryPeople Press
113 E. Water St.
Decorah, IA 52101
USA

866.564.4552
563.382.8932
563.382.0263 FAX

StoryPeople
P.O. Box 7
Decorah, IA 52101
USA

800.476.7178
563.382.8060
563.382.0263 FAX